THE PHILOSOPHY OF
COCKTAILS

THE PHILOSOPHY OF
COCKTAILS

JANE PEYTON

First published 2023 by
The British Library
96 Euston Road
London NW1 2DB

ISBN 978 0 7123 5453 0
eISBN 978 0 7123 6806 3
Cataloguing in Publication Data
A catalogue record for this book is available
from the British Library

Designed and typeset by Sandra Friesen
Printed in the Czech Republic by Finidr

MIX
Paper | Supporting
responsible forestry
FSC
www.fsc.org
FSC® C014138

CONTENTS

INTRODUCTION

The Drinks Cabinet

MY FRIEND MIKE in Los Angeles is a cocktail devotee who regularly sends text messages with menus from bars he has visited and photographs of what he is drinking. Because of the time difference between LA and Britain (home), they usually arrive after my phone is switched on in the morning, meaning that I start the day with a cocktail, albeit a virtual one. Without fail Mike's messages remind me of how alcoholic drinks unite people throughout the world. They also confirm the wonderment and intrigue of cocktails. To me they are the liquid definition of the idiom 'greater than the sum of its parts'. I like to sip neat spirits, in particular gin, whisky and rum, but when mixed with vermouth, bitters, or lime juice and mint leaves, then garnished, they are transformed into magical potions with names such as Martini, Manhattan and Mojito. A cocktail is never just about the liquid itself; it is also about the ritual and the transportive nature of the libation that adds a sparkle to how we feel in that moment.

All the components in a cocktail are sourced from foodstuffs so the person making it is the equivalent of a chef combining ingredients to create a whole. Mixologists are magicians, and creating cocktails is theatre where the props are the shaker, the stirrer, the jigger, the strainer, the garnish and the glassware, followed by the big reveal.

Another Los Angeles-based friend, Marc, describes his enjoyment of creating cocktails at home as: 'Cocktail mixing time marks a shift in the day and a change of mindset. It means relaxing, pampering myself and being a little self-indulgent. The process is fun, going through the steps, getting proportions right, choosing the correct glass and garnish, and hopefully ending with something that tastes good.'

I was familiar with cocktails before I ever ordered one because my music playlist included Sarah Vaughan singing of a cool Mint Julep on a summery day in 'You Hit the Spot', and Nancy Wilson who offered to fix a quick Martini in 'Guess Who I Saw Today'. When I visited New York City and sat in the bar of the Algonquin hotel, I followed Julie London's lead by asking the barman to 'make it another Old Fashioned, please', as she had done in the song of the same name. It felt very grown-up, sophisticated and appropriate for the location. My very first cocktail, or so I thought until writing this book. What was that gin and lime I used to

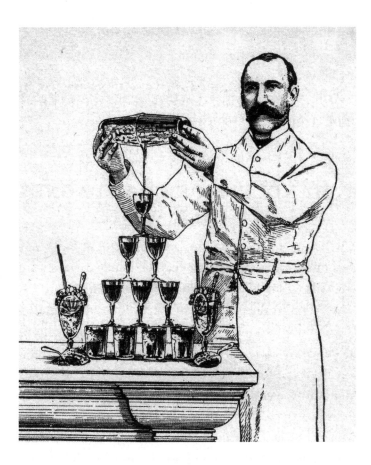

order as a newly legal tippler in the Black Horse pub if not a Gimlet, and those teenage house parties where the greatest return on investment for speed of intoxication came in the guise of a bottle of red vermouth? 'Wonder what it would taste like with some of this?' I said as we raided the pantry and found a bottle of Gordon's. By doing so we had unwittingly created Gin & It, following the age-old habit of *Homo sapiens* experimenting with what is available to create something to sup.

What is a cocktail? According to the *Oxford English Dictionary* there are two definitions:

☞ A drink usually made from a mixture of one or more spirits.

☞ A mix of different elements or substances, usually ones that do not mix well together.

As I outline in the following chapter, human beings were enjoying cocktails millennia before the advent of spiritous liquors, so for the purposes of this book I am expanding the definition to include any blended alcoholic or non-alcoholic beverage.

Cocktail history abounds with myths, maybes and claims about provenance that cannot always be proven, but it is clear that the earliest recorded use of the word 'cocktail' with a connection to alcohol was in a 1798 London newspaper, although the etymology is confused. There are several theories behind the word's origin, and these are the most plausible:

1. 'Cock-tailings', the dregs at the bottom of barrels in British hostelries, were mingled and sold at a discount.

2. A common practice with mixed-breed horses was to dock their tail, which then resembled a cockerel's fan tail. Cocktails are mixed drinks, so it relates to cross-bred horses.
3. Another horse connection is the now discredited practice of inserting a piece of ginger root into the anus of an old horse. It would cock its tail in shock and could be passed off to potential buyers as a younger, livelier creature.
4. It was a mispronunciation of the old French word for a mixed drink, *coquetel*, or the French term for an eggcup, *coquetier*, which was used in bars for measuring liquid.

This book looks at the factors that influenced the development and popularity of cocktails, so it starts with prehistoric potations, then examines the use of distillation to create alcohol for medicinal consumption; it looks at how colonisation spread the habit of imbibing spirits for recreation, as well as the influence of politics and world events on cocktail culture, and how the drinks were glamorised. America and Britain had the biggest impact, so the focus is on those two nations.

Some of popular culture's most unforgettable characters are indelibly connected with cocktails. Carrie Bradshaw is also a wine drinker, but we think of her ordering Cosmopolitans with her friends at fashionable New York venues in the TV series *Sex and the City*; James Bond quaffs beer too, but we associate him with the Martini and picture him wearing an elegant dinner jacket in the casino at Monte Carlo.

Cocktails are served in the world's most stylish bars and it is hard to believe they are the progeny of the mixed beverages crafted by humans thousands of years ago, but they are. So, fill a shaker with your favourite mix, give it a stir, and raise a glass to the ancestors.

IN THE BEGINNING

WHEN ARCHAEOLOGISTS from Penn State University unearthed a tomb in the central Turkey region formerly known as Phrygia, they saw gold, which was appropriate, for this was the resting place of King Midas (or possibly his father, Gordius; no one is sure). The gold, actually bronze, was an astounding discovery and formed the largest set of Iron Age drinking vessels ever found, comprising 157 bowls, jugs and vats, some of which were decorated with the heads of lions and rams.

Decades after the 1957 excavation, biomolecular archaeologist Dr Patrick McGovern analysed residue present on the metal. Organic markers revealed a blend of grape wine, barley beer, and mead (fermented honey), which was probably left over from the king's funerary feast. Midas (or Gordius) had been interred, *circa* 740 BCE, with a supply of cocktails to refresh him in the afterlife.

It was not just the Phrygians who were partial to that concoction; researchers have studied archaeological material from sites in Crete and mainland Greece dating to approximately 1600 BCE which contained similar constituents – a mixture of wine, barley and honey with a garnish of goat's cheese grated on top. That combination was called *kykeon* and is mentioned in Homer's *Odyssey* when Circe, an enchantress, tempts Odysseus and his companions to swig it to the point of stupefaction, after which she transmutes them to pigs.

Wine, beer and mead have been consumed for millennia, and the earliest archaeological proof (7000 BCE) is in deposits on pottery from Jiahu, a neolithic village in north-central China. In addition to honey, rice beer and grapes, there was another fruit, possibly hawthorn. Did news of this type of drink transfer westwards through migration and trade, or were humans using what they could locate in their region to make intoxicants but with no knowledge of other cultures doing the same? It is likely to have been both. Mixed drinks were common in antiquity because successful fermentation required additional sources of sugar. They may also have been tastier with multiple ingredients. Archaeo-botanical remains in the grave of a woman in Denmark buried sometime between 1500 and 1300 BCE comprised mead, beer, fruit and flowers. In Peru the fermented fruit of the Peruvian pepper tree, which in the Quechua language translates as 'tree of life', was combined with corn malt and cactus and cornstalk juices. Palm wine from dates or tree sap has an ancient pedigree in tropical and sub-tropical Africa, and 18,000-year-old evidence from southern Egypt offers the

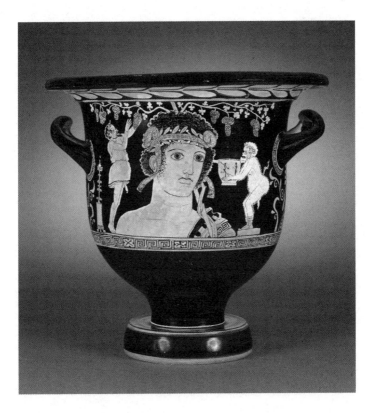

tantalising theory that wild lily, chamomile, tubers and wild grains might have been blended with it.

Anthropologists believe hominids purposely started drinking during the Palaeolithic era after becoming mildly intoxicated from eating overripe fruit, which unbeknown to them was fermenting. Speculation about what they were quaffing is necessary because provisions were stored in vessels made of organic material that left no archaeological

trace. Ripe fruit stored in a container would partially pulp, prompting yeast cells on the skins to ferment it. Observation and experimentation led to fruit being pressed for juice so it became an alcoholic drink rather than an alcoholic mush. Meanwhile someone collecting honey might have noticed a stash in the crack of a tree trunk soaked by rainfall. Rain diluted the sugar so airborne wild yeast was able to ferment it. Whichever inquisitive person tasted the liquid had their first experience of mead. It was delicious and gave them a gentle buzz. Eventually they worked out that by adding water to honey and waiting a few days it would be transformed, and by downing generous amounts they were transported to an altered state.

When *Homo sapiens* moved north out of Africa, beginning around 100,000 BCE, they had the knowledge to create a drinks menu from a plethora of edibles. Alcohol is liquid food and it supplied essential calories and energy in an environment where resources were not always easily available. Fermentation enhances the nutritional value of food through the process of biological ennoblement, and not only is it more nutritious, but it contains microflora which, among other benefits, maintain healthy intestines and boost immune system functions. People who drank alcohol were hardier than the abstemious, and arguably less reserved, as its psychoactive effects caused them to be cheerful and sociable.

As late as the mid-nineteenth century, when scientist Louis Pasteur confirmed the role of yeast in converting sugar to alcohol, there was still a widespread belief that the transformation of food was supernatural. For thousands of years alcohol was used in pagan worship, and deities were associated with specific libations; for instance, Ninkasi in Sumer (modern-day Iraq) for beer, and Bacchus in ancient Rome for wine. Some societies believed alcohol was sacred and contained godly essence, and veneration of the associated divinities entailed great public feasts where visible intoxication was expected. Even today in Judaism and some Christian faiths wine is used in holy rites and cited in the scriptures as God given.

Alcohol is a social lubricant used to build community bonds, seal contracts, assist negotiations, resolve disagreements, celebrate significant events and enable people to have fun. Its effects are seductive because when the body absorbs small doses the brain releases dopamine, serotonin and opioid neurotransmitters, causing elation and pleasure. Those chemicals also stimulate the brain's emotional centres, particularly the ones connected with language and inhibition. Another neural area affected by alcohol is the limbic system, which controls responses including arousal, motivations and reminiscence. Alcohol's aroma taps into memory storage and retrieval and reminds us of good or bad times on the booze. The aversion some people have to the smell of tequila because they flashback to a terrible hangover is directly related to the limbic system.

Humankind might be hardwired to seek intoxication. Alcohol is just one way of achieving that state; love, religion, drugs, dancing, music and psychotropic plants can do the same. Throughout history it has been part of the human experience, and even now the reasons for imbibing are remarkably similar to what they were in the beginning.

SEARCHING
FOR IMMORTALITY

SOME PEOPLE WHO eschew gin because of its heady aromatics may feel vindicated to know that distillation was originally employed to make perfume, not alcohol.

Distillation, from the Latin *destillare*, meaning 'to drip', is a method of separating components in liquid by boiling and condensation. With a spirit, concentrated ethanol (alcohol) is derived by heating fermented fruits (wine), cereals (beer), root crops, sap, vegetables and other natural sources of sugar. Ethanol evaporates at a lower temperature than the rest of the liquid, and if the collected steam is cooled, it condenses into a high-strength liquor.

At its simplest, the necessary equipment is a pot with a lid in which to boil the substance, an enclosed space where the vapours accumulate, and a bowl to collect the trickles of condensate. To date the earliest apparatus consisting of those three pieces was unearthed in Mesopotamia (modern-day Iraq) dating back to approximately 3500 BCE. Although archaeologists cannot confirm the exact use, it is likely to have been for perfumed waters. Inscriptions on Babylonian clay tablets (also modern-day Iraq) *circa* 1200 BCE describe the operations of a perfumery. Knowledge of distillation developed, and by the third century BCE alchemists in Egypt, Greece, Rome and China were using it to convert seawater to potable water, and to manufacture balms and medicinal essences. Crucially for the development of spirituous liquors, testing of wine was also undertaken, as revealed by first-century Roman naturalist Pliny, who wrote: 'By some mode or other it was discovered that water itself might be made to intoxicate.' He was referring to the colourless condensate that resulted from heating wine, which with the basic distilling technology of the time would have been lower in strength than contemporary spirits, although still potent.

Even though the intoxicating nature of distilled wine was recognised, it was not used recreationally because alchemists had other priorities. They were seeking a method to convert base metals such as nickel into high-value noble metals including gold and silver. That never happened, but the search for a panacea capable of curing disease was more successful. It took over a millennium before academics believed they had accomplished their mythical quest when they referred to distilled wine as *aqua vita*, meaning 'the water of life'.

Establishing a comprehensive timeline is impossible due to lack of written and archaeological records, no standard language for the discipline of distilling and, crucially, no word for alcohol itself. Although it was apparent something magical happened to wine, no one understood the process. Extensive research into the distillation of liquids by chemists in Baghdad during the eighth and ninth centuries enhanced understanding, but the subject was still very much a mystery. Persian alchemist Abu Musa Jabir ibn Hayyan, aka Geber, advanced distilling techniques with his innovative alembic still. He noted that distilled wine generated flammable vapour, not knowing it was alcoholic spirit, and described it as 'of little use but of great importance to science'.

Spirits were still not being quaffed for merriment, and the description by eighth-century Arab poet Abu Nuwas of an unidentified liquid, but most probably alcohol, as 'the colour of rainwater and hot inside the ribs as a burning firebrand' was hardly a convincing sales pitch.

Forward 400 years to Europe, where texts from chemists and academics in Italy and France outlined their search for the elixir of life from distilled wine, which they labelled *aqua vita*. Arnaldus de Villa Nova, thirteenth-century physician, wrote of it as *eau de vie*: 'It prolongs life, and therefore deserves to be called water of life.' Taddeo Alderotti, an academic in mid-thirteenth-century Florence, pronounced it 'the parent and lord of all medicines and its effects are marvellous'. Professor Alderotti is also credited with improving fractional distillation, which separates liquids of different boiling points, leading to high-strength

WHAT'S IN A NAME?

Where did the names of the world's major spirits originate?

ABSINTHE: A French aniseed-flavoured spirit that also contains leaves and flowers of the wormwood plant, Latin name *Artemisia absinthium*. In the early twentieth century several countries temporarily banned it in the mistaken belief that because wormwood contained the compound thujone, absinthe was a psychoactive drug that caused hallucinations.

BRANDY: A corruption of the Dutch phrase *gebrande wijn*, which translates as 'burned wine', brandy is distilled fermented grape or other fruit juice. Cognac and Armagnac are types of French brandy named after the regions in which they are made. Pisco is brandy distilled in Peru and Chile from the fermented juice of specific grapes. Grappa is Italian brandy but uses grape pomace – leftover skins, seeds and stalks from wine production.

GIN: The name evolved in the seventeenth century from genever, a popular spirit in the Low Countries

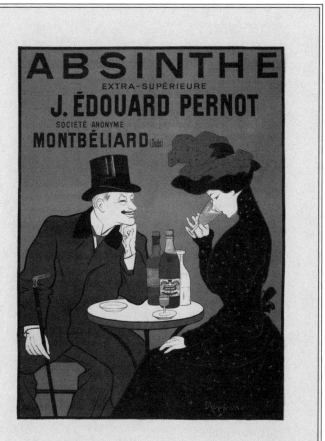

(modern-day Netherlands and Belgium). When genever (pronounced in English as 'jenneever') became prevalent in England, its nickname was Madam Geneva, hence the shortened form, gin.

The spirit is a distillate of fermented cereal, potato, beet or fruit, which is flavoured with juniper, citrus, herbs, spices and other botanicals. There are several types: Old Tom, with a malty and subtle sweetness; Plymouth, an earthy style from the eponymous English town; and London dry. This can be produced anywhere, not just in London, but is a legal definition and nothing apart from diluting water may be added after distillation.

RUM: Distilled fermented molasses, a by-product of white sugar production. In its early days, rum went by the names rumbullion, rumbustion and rumbowling. The etymology is not clear but two plausible explanations are that it came from *Saccharum officinarum*, Latin for sugar cane, or that it is a corruption of *bram* or *brum*, Malay words for distilled sugar cane juice. Rhum Agricole, a style which originated in French Caribbean islands, is made by distilling fermented sugar cane juice.

TEQUILA: A type of mezcal which, to qualify as genuine, must be produced by juicing and fermenting the baked core of the blue agave plant in the Mexican municipalities of Tequila or Arandas.

Mezcal does not have a geographic restriction to its production. The name mezcal derives from the Nahuatl language, where *metl* translates as agave and *ixcalli* as cooked.

WHISKY: An anglicised version of *uisge beatha* (pronounced 'ishky baa'), the Scottish Gaelic phrase for 'water of life'. In Ireland and the USA, the spelling is whiskey. Whisk(e)y is created by fermenting barley, wheat, rye or corn, then ageing the distillate in wooden barrels, in the case of Scotch for at least three years and a day. Bourbon is a type of American whiskey which must, by law, be crafted from no less than 51 per cent fermented corn.

VODKA: A diminutive of *voda*, the Russian term for water. Both Russia and Poland claim they were the pioneers of vodka, although Poland has more written evidence to support the assertion. Polish documents from the fifteenth century refer to *wódka* when it was taken as a medicinal tincture, and *gorzeć* when it was consumed recreationally. Vodka is made by fermenting cereal, potato, fruit, or lactose from milk, which is then distilled.

pure alcohol, which begat the nickname *aqua ardens*, or in English 'ardent or burning waters'.

One of the most influential paeans to the power of *aqua vita* was compiled by Hieronymus Brunschwig, a fifteenth-century Strasbourg-born medic. In *Liber de arte distillandi de simplicibus* ('the little book of distillation') he called it 'the mistress of medicines that comforts the heart … It heals baldness and causes the hair well to grow, and kills lice and fleas. It cures lethargy … It causes good digestions and appetite for to eat, and takes away belching … It purifies the five wits of melancholy and of all uncleanness.'

The opinion that *aqua vita* was indeed a miraculous wonder drug to benefit all manner of ailments prevailed not least because herbs and spices are soluble in ethanol, so their active ingredients enter the bloodstream effectively. It revolutionised medicine. Manufacturers of *aqua vita* started supplying directly to the public, and the wealthy employed distillers on their staff. In Scotland, accounting records from King James IV's household in 1499 reveal the purchase of *aqua vita* (one of the first references to what in that country became better known as whisky) and several years later the monarch granted a monopoly on production to the Guild of Surgeons and Barbers.

Ardent waters now had a dual role of being integral to the medicine cabinet, and as a libation for recreation and intoxication, but if anyone was writing contemporaneously about the fun aspect of tippling, the reports did not survive. One of the oldest references to *aqua vita* (probably whisky) being a social nip is in the musings of English poet John Taylor, who in 1618 published *The Pennyles Pilgrimage* outlining his epic journey travelling on foot from London to Scotland and, with no money, relying on the hospitality of people he met along the way. For one overnight lodging he wrote of being offered a smorgasbord of game, fish and poultry, and '... good ale, sack [sherry] white, and claret, tent [red wine from southern Spain] with most potent *aqua vita*'. His hosts were far from stingy!

As the wondrous reputation of distillate spread, people experimented with their local fermented beverage. In India that was from mahua and kadamba flowers; in Korea soju from rice; and in Mexico agave to make mezcal. In Poland, Sweden and Russia, where grain was distilled, the *aqua vita* was vodka, and in Holland juniper and spices were added to create genever (the Dutch word for juniper), which, when distilled in England, became known as gin.

We joke about alcohol being what the doctor ordered, but three of today's classic cocktails had therapeutic use when they originated in the eighteenth and nineteenth centuries. All of them contained gin, and its primary ingredient, juniper, had been used for millennia to treat myriad health conditions. Two, the Pink Gin and the Gimlet, were born aboard British naval ships which carried spirits as a painkiller, anaesthetic, sterilant, antiseptic and as part of the crew's daily rations.

Bitters are a concentrated gallimaufry of herbs, spices, bark, seeds and roots long used as medicinal elixirs and marketed as cure-alls. Ship doctors included them in the medicine chest as a treatment for, among other things, seasickness, and when mingled with gin they imbued a delicate rose colour, giving rise to Pink Gin. The Gimlet, a simple fusion of gin and lime juice, was an effective prophylactic against the scourge of scurvy. Caused by vitamin C deficiency, scurvy is deadly when left untreated. Mariners on months-long voyages with limited stores of fresh food were susceptible, so when, towards the end of the eighteenth century, the British Admiralty realised citrus was the elusive cure, sailors were prescribed a compulsory daily dose of lemon or lime juice (the source of the nickname 'Limeys'). Someone spiked it with a tot of gin and invented the Gimlet, its name possibly stemming from the term for a metal tool used to drill a hole in the juice barrel.

Of the three medicinal cocktails, the most significant is arguably Gin & Tonic, most likely devised in India. Quinine, sourced from the bark of *Cinchona officinalis*, aka the fever tree, is a treatment for malaria and works by killing the parasite responsible for the disease and calming malarial symptoms. Chemists working in 1820 isolated water-soluble quinine sulphate, which was exceptionally bitter, but less so with gin, and when carbonated tonic water containing quinine was commercialised in the mid-nineteenth century, it was a perfect mixer. With the addition of a lemon slice and chunks of ice, what would become the world's most widely consumed cocktail was born.

PICK AND MIX

Several cocktails on contemporary menus existed before cocktails were defined by an American newspaper in 1806 as being 'a stimulating liquor, composed of spirits of any kind, sugar, water, and bitters'. Step forward the julep, flip, sling, punch and toddy. Of those, toddy has the oldest origin, India, from the late sixteenth century, and its name possibly derived from *todi*, Hindi for 'a drink from fermented palm sap'. Like so many notions prior to modern communications, trade assisted the dissemination of ideas and practices, and when the toddy reached Britain in the early seventeenth century, it had been modified with sugar and spices, hot water and any available liquor. Across the Atlantic, American colonists and settlers in the Caribbean perked up theirs with rum or whiskey, and even in muggy climes they were in demand because warm beverages draw heat from the body by producing sweat. By the nineteenth century, a hot toddy also included honey and lemon juice, and was a folk cure for the common cold. Warm liquids ease nasal congestion, spices stimulate the production of saliva, which eases a sore throat, vitamin C from lemon juice strengthens the immune system when used long term, honey protects the throat from irritation by coating it with a soothing layer, and the added whisk(e)y, brandy or rum has a painkilling effect. As the Ukrainian proverb says: 'Drink a glass of wine after your soup and you will be stealing a rouble from the doctor', endorsing thousands of years of alcohol being used medicinally.

Another pick-me-up is the flip. Now it contains a spirit or fortified wine plus sugar, and a whole egg, shaken with ice and garnished with grated nutmeg, but it started as a mix of sweet warm ale, rum, brandy or whisky, dunked with a red-hot poker to make it froth. Flips were consumed in England from at least the seventeenth century and introduced into America, where eventually the ale was replaced by a raw egg, and by the late nineteenth century it was mostly served chilled. Whether Charles Dickens was referring to the warm or cold version is not clear when he wrote of sharing 'a jug of mellow flip' at the Six Jolly Fellowship Porters pub in the novel *Our Mutual Friend*.

Dickens was also well acquainted with punch, which he mentioned in *A Christmas Carol* and *David Copperfield*. Not only that but he was adept at mixing it when hosting parties, combining storytelling and theatrical flair, especially when flaming his blend of rum, brandy, lemon juice, sugar and hot water. Punch is now out of fashion, but for at least 200 years it was the intoxicant

of choice for social gatherings by the English middle and
upper classes, a convivial potation dispensed from large
decorative porcelain, glass or metal bowls and ladled into
individual punch cups. Its current reputation as a tame and
old-fashioned refreshment sipped only by genteel people
such as guests at the Netherfield ball in Jane Austen's
Pride and Prejudice is inaccurate because it was not just
Elizabeth Bennet who enjoyed a cup; so did Captain Kidd.
Yes, pirates were keen on rum punch, and it was sold in
taverns on Caribbean islands. London in the eighteenth
and nineteenth centuries had dedicated punch-houses,
notorious for their raucous atmosphere, where groups of

SWITCHELS AND SHRUBS

When wine is pronounced worthy only as salad dressing, it is generally not a compliment. Vinegar is meant for the condiment cupboard, not as a beverage, isn't it? Well, no, as it turns out, because water-diluted vinegar-based drinks with added spices or fruit have been consumed for millennia. In pre-revolutionary America, molasses and ginger were added to vinegar, and the mixes were known as switchels.

A shrub is a concoction of fruit or vegetables macerated in vinegar and flavoured with botanicals. The name comes from the early Arabic *sharāb*, meaning 'to drink'. Another version of the word is 'sherbet', a colloquialism for an alcoholic nip. In England the shrub changed from a fifteenth-century medicinal cordial comprising brandy, sugar and citrus juice into a fruit liqueur sold in pubs, and if citrus was unavailable, it was replaced with vinegar for acidity. Colonial America embraced vinegar shrubs and changed them to syrups for mixing with liquor, or diluted them with water for non-intoxicating refreshment. Today they have a dual purpose as a soft drink and, with their concentrated flavours, super-enhancers for cocktails. To prove it, Nonsuch Shrubs created the spicy and warming ECT cocktail especially for this book.

THE ECT

Ingredients

50 ml bourbon
25 ml Nonsuch Caramelised
Pineapple & Ginger Shrub
30 ml soda water
Dash of bitters

Method

Add the bourbon and shrub to a cocktail shaker with ice. Shake vigorously. Strain over ice into a short tumbler, add the soda water and bitters, then stir.

FROM MIXED DRINK
TO DESSERT

Syllabub is now a dessert of whipped cream with sherry or fortified wine and sugar, but initially it was beer and cider combined with warm milk, ideally fresh from a cow. A recipe in *The Experienced English Housewife* by Elizabeth Raffald, published in 1769, described how to make a syllabub 'under the cow': 'Put a bottle of strong beer and a pint of cider into a punch bowl, grate in a small nutmeg and sweeten it to your taste. Then milk as much milk from the cow as will make a strong froth … Let it stand an hour, then strew over it a few currants well washed, picked, and plumped before the fire. Then send it to the table.'

Another creamy dessert that evolved from a mixed drink is the posset, prepared in England from at least the sixteenth century and often taken as a restorative for colds and fevers. It consisted of sweetened warm curdled milk with fortified wine.

William Shakespeare mentions the posset in plays including *Macbeth* (Act 2, Scene 2) where the grooms outside King Duncan's quarters sleep through the regicide because Lady Macbeth spiked their drinks: 'The doors are open, and the surfeited grooms do mock their charge with snores: I have drugged their possets.'

MR. MICAWBER IN HIS ELEMENT.

men gathered to quaff and misbehave because, as the name suggests, it packed a punch.

Punch came from India and was popularised by British sailors and traders returning home. A letter sent in 1632 by an employee of the East India Company wrote of his new life in the subcontinent and how he hoped to have plenty of punch to imbibe. There are two theories about the word's etymology. One that it derives from the Sanskrit *pancha*, meaning five, and relates to the number of ingredients in the mix, and the other, from noted cocktail historian David Wondrich, that it stems from 'puncheon', a specific size of wooden barrel for storing alcohol.

Punch lends itself to freestyling with the formulation, and one nourishing version was milk punch. In *The Compleat Housewife: Or, Accomplish'd Gentlewoman's Companion*, published 1727 in London and later a bestseller in America, author Eliza Smith includes her recipe: '… Take two quarts of water, one quart of milk, half a pint of lemon juice, and one quart of brandy, sugar to your taste. Put the milk and water together a little warm, then the sugar, then the lemon juice, stir it well together, then the brandy, stir it again and run through a flannel bag till 'tis very fine, then bottle it; it will keep a fortnight, or more.'

From England and the Caribbean, punch moved on to the American colonies where, because of easy access to rum, it turned into a staple. One of its attractions was the communal act of imbibing to build bonds, seal business deals and celebrate. A similar drink was the sling, and it consisted of any choice of spirit, fruit juice, sugar and water. Unlike punch, which was prepared in volume, the sling was a single-serve mixture.

Just as punch is associated with England but originated elsewhere, the julep is indelibly seen as American, except that it too has its roots in another country. Juleps developed in the Middle East and found a home in America, where they became a stalwart of the cocktail canon. Mint Julep is the familiar version and was prominent in the southern United States from 1770, when it was cited in print as being medicinal because mint is anti-inflammatory, clears

PURLY QUEEN

Purl was the medieval name for English ale combined with wormwood and was taken as a purgative. It transformed into mulled ale, with gin, sugar and spices, and by the middle of the nineteenth century was popular in the USA, where purl houses also sold posset, punch and other nascent cocktails. Purl Royal substituted wine for ale.

respiratory congestion, has antibacterial and antiseptic properties, and relieves indigestion.

The name, from ancient Persian *gulāb* (also written as *julāb*), where *gul* meant rose and *āb* water, was mentioned in a text from 900 CE and described a non-alcoholic draft of violets in sweetened water. Violets were used as a remedy for numerous ailments such as sore throats, digestive problems and high blood pressure. Therapeutic use of the julep spread west, and in England Dr Samuel Johnson, who in 1755 published the first Dictionary of the English Language, defined a 'julap' as an 'extemporaneous form of medicine made of simple and compound water sweetened'. Dr Johnson does not mention alcohol, but knowing how

apothecaries included it in so many treatments, it is unlikely English juleps were soft drinks.

Settlers took the julep habit to America and, with the addition of ice in the late-eighteenth century, it had all the curative benefits of mint, plus being a go-to refreshment for cooling down in hot weather. A modern Mint Julep has barely altered since its inception in the USA and consists of liquor (usually bourbon), sugar muddled with mint, and crushed ice. Simple and effective.

OLD WORLD TO
NEW WORLD

SPIRITS ARE THE foundation of cocktails and although they were enthusiastically imbibed in the Old World, it was in the New World that their consumption had such an impact on history. It started in the fifteenth century when sugar cane plants were transported to the new Portuguese colony of Brazil, but at that time there could have been no inkling of the consequences that would result. Sugar cane was probably domesticated in Papua New Guinea around 8000 BCE. Cultivation then moved to Southeast Asia and China and, later, East and North Africa, Lebanon and Spain to feed a burgeoning addiction to the exotic luxury known in Europe as 'sweet salt'. Even that was not enough, hence the establishment of south American plantations in Brazil and Atlantic coastal land. Christopher Columbus introduced sugar cane seedlings to Cuba and Hispaniola in 1493, and by 1501 successful harvests confirmed the region had a perfect climate for the crop to flourish. Caribbean islands seized by the Spanish, French and British navies were prime locations for cultivating what came to be called 'white gold'. Sugar production was the equivalent of printing money and amassed vast fortunes for landowners who abandoned tobacco and cotton to concentrate on the more valuable commodity. But sourcing enough labourers to work in its production meant enslaving the indigenous population, using prisoners of war and indentured servants, and over the centuries trafficking millions of men, women and children, mostly from Africa, into slavery.

Molasses is a by-product of white sugar production. The name stems from the Portuguese *melaço*, which in turn derives from *mel*, Latin for honey. It had negligible monetary value and was used as fertiliser, or fed to animals. When someone unknown to history, possibly on the island of Nevis, distilled fermented molasses in the seventeenth century, they created a type of rum emblematic of the West Indies. It was not the first sugar-based spirit, however, because arrack distilled from fermented cane had been produced in Southeast Asia since the twelfth century and was mentioned in the memoirs of explorer Marco Polo. In Brazil, *aguardente*, aka 'burning water', was also distilled from cane juice and is the mother of cachaça, the country's national liquor and base of the Caipirinha cocktail. Barbadian rum from molasses was mentioned in a letter of 1647, where it was described as 'kill devil' on account of its harsh quality and potential for prodigious hangovers. Pursers on visiting British ships purchased rum for onboard medical use, and sailors received a half-pint as

Fourneaux 3.Formes. 4.Vinaigrerie. 5.Cannes SVCRERIE. 6.Grue. 7.Latanir. 8.Papinirioba. 9.Choux. 10.Cafes. 11.Figure
Chaudieres. de Juice Choux; &c. r. 111. r. 12. Carmibes. de Negres.

their daily ration instead of the usual gallon of ale or pint of wine. To prevent scurvy, citrus juice was added to grog, a drink of watered-down rum, probably named after 'Old Grog', the soubriquet of Vice-Admiral Edward Vernon, who had worked to improve naval procedures and was known for wearing a grogram cloth greatcoat.

By the early eighteenth century rum was so profitable that every Barbadian planter who could afford distilling equipment was producing and selling what was dubbed 'rumbustion' or 'rumbullion'. Plantation owners on other Caribbean islands and in South American mainland colonies capitalised on molasses to make a rough and ready distillate worthy of the contemporaneous description

of 'a hot, hellish and terrible liquor'. With so much competition the distillers of Barbados finessed their rum to make it more palatable by adding water to reduce the strength and ageing it in oak barrels to soften it.

In America's New England colonies, rum was the favourite hooch, and thanks to a local workforce skilled in metalworking and barrel cooperage, an abundant source of lumber, a regular supply of molasses from the West Indies and 140-plus distilleries, rum production became one of the largest industries, accounting for 80 per cent of exports. Rum was so much in demand, Native Americans accepted it as currency when trading furs, and it replaced French brandy as the preferred method of payment in the purchase of enslaved Africans. This led to a triangular trade where molasses imported from the West Indies to New England was distilled into rum that was exported to West Africa in exchange for humans trafficked to the West Indies. When France banned its New World territories from producing rum, to protect the domestic brandy sector from alternative sources of liquor, molasses on French Caribbean islands was all but worthless and sold cut-price to New Englanders. Mother England was not amused that its colonial offspring were trading with the enemy, France, and this led to the Molasses Act 1733, which levied a prohibitive tax on molasses sourced from suppliers other than those in British-ruled lands. This was followed in 1764 by the Sugar Act, which taxed rum, molasses and Madeira wine imported into the American colony. Relations with the old country were already deteriorating, and taxation without representation was intolerable. Drastic action was required. The Declaration of Independence signed in 1776 was celebrated by the Founding Fathers with dozens of bowls of rum punch, and one of the signatories, John Adams, said, 'I know not why we should blush to confess that molasses was an essential ingredient in American independence.' Rum fortified the revolutionary soldiers led by George Washington, who issued a daily ration to the troops and wrote, 'The benefits arising from the moderate use of strong liquor have been experienced in all armies and are not to be disputed.'

Male citizens of the new republic were big boozers and the hard stuff was central, not just to social life but to business transactions and politics. Electoral candidates bought votes by giving away liquor at rallies and the electorate expected to be bribed for their support. A tight-fisted contender had no chance of success. Alcohol had been fundamental to the lives of Americans ever since the Puritans arrived in 1620. To them, it was sanctioned by the Almighty, and a preacher named Increase Mather wrote that 'Drink is in itself a good creature of God, and to be received with thankfulness.' However, he went on to warn that 'the abuse of drink is from Satan', which was largely ignored as the colonies expanded because many people drank throughout the day and it was acceptable to have a

THE DRINKER'S
DICTIONARY

In 1737, Benjamin Franklin, American writer, inventor, diplomat and Founding Father, wrote an article for the *Pennsylvania Gazette* which included a list of 230 phrases for being drunk. He explained (with his original spelling and capital-isation): 'The Phrases in this Dictionary are not borrow'd from Foreign Languages, neither are they collected from the Writings of the Learned in our own, but gather'd wholly from the modern Tavern-Conversation of Tiplers ...'

This is a selection:

Afflicted, Biggy, Bewitch'd, Burdock'd, His Head is full of Bees, He's had a Thump over the Head with Sampson's Jawbone, Cherubimical, Wamble Crop'd, Crack'd, He's been too free with the Creature, Wet both Eyes, He's Eat a Toad & half for Breakfast, Got on his little Hat, Loose in the Hilts, Jambled, Moon-Ey'd, Nimptopsical, Oxycrocium, Pungey, Double Tongu'd, Has Swallow'd a Tavern Token.

morning pick-me-up, followed by a lunchtime dram, and an afternoon freshener before the evening's serious boozing. In addition to boundless supplies of rum, there was no shortage of brandy thanks to the plethora of locally grown apples, peaches, cherries and other fruits. And then there was whiskey. Scottish and Irish immigrants brought with them the quaffing habits and necessary skills to make their national drink, and with crude home stills and own-grown cereal, distilling became an important cottage industry, a symbol of self-sufficiency in the new nation. In the absence of a healthcare system, whiskey was the answer. Nineteenth-century travelling medicine shows combined entertainment from acrobats, freak shows and magicians with the peddling of patent medicines and miracle cures that, along with various botanicals, had the same secret ingredient: whiskey.

When a glut of corn meant it was more profitable converted to whiskey than traded as cereal, over-supply resulted in a price drop until, at 25 cents a gallon, it was cheaper than beer or milk. Not surprisingly, consumption increased. Spirits soaked every aspect of life in the new republic, as Frederick Marryat, English novelist travelling in the USA, wrote in his 1837 *A Diary in America*:

I am sure the Americans can fix nothing without a drink. If you meet, you drink; if you part, you drink; if you make acquaintance, you drink; if you close a bargain you drink; they quarrel in their drink, and they make it up with a

drink. They drink because it is hot; they drink because it is cold. If successful in elections, they drink and rejoice; if not, they drink and swear; they begin to drink early in the morning, they leave off late at night; they commence it early in life and they continue it, until they soon drop into the grave.

Given America's love affair with spiritous liquors, their easy availability and their everyday status, it is fitting that the advancement of cocktails should commence there. But for them to become what we now recognise it needed showmen with theatrical flair. Let's meet the mixologists.

MIXING IT UP

'GOOD EVENING SIR, what can I get you?' asked the waiter in the bar of New York's Metropolitan Hotel.

'Whiskey Sour,' the customer replied, lighting a cigar.

This was the mid-1860s and his drink was about to be prepared by Jeremiah 'Jerry' Thomas, nicknamed 'The Professor' for his ability to formulate his own infusions, and the knowledge and creative skills he displayed in his work. Thomas is the father of modern bartending, not least because he published the profession's inaugural guidebook, *How to Mix Drinks, or The Bon Vivant's Companion* (1862). It comprised numerous recipes for the customary toddies, punches and slings, plus ten concoctions referred to as cocktails. What differentiated a cocktail from the others was the inclusion of bitters, but by the end of the century cocktail came to mean liquor and a mixer whether it contained bitters or not. Jerry Thomas codified the elements of cocktails, which meant people could order a particular drink in San Francisco or Singapore and bartenders would know how to make it.

Until his book was published, recipes were mostly verbally shared and there was no standardisation.

The Professor pioneered 'flair bartending' where the bartender spins bottles, juggles glasses and flips jiggers, all in the cause of entertaining customers. If his techniques were considered flamboyant, his bar tools, solid silver encrusted with precious stones, were even more so. He wore tailored jackets, starched collars and crisp white shirts with diamond tie pin and cufflinks, and his charismatic personality was as much a draw, bringing theatre to whatever he did, most memorably when he was accompanied by two pet white rats on his shoulders as he worked. His signature cocktail was the Blue Blazer, a combination of Scotch whisky, sugar and hot water, which he set on fire, transferring the liquid between two metal tumblers to create a rainbow of flame. With his star power he was much in demand not only in the USA but Europe too. Everywhere Thomas went he was an ambassador who elevated cocktails as something more than just an agreeable intoxicating drink.

Jerry Thomas's legacy as one of the architects of the golden age of cocktails is undisputed. It was an era that lasted roughly from 1860 to the beginning of the Second World War and includes Prohibition in the USA, which, despite booze being outlawed, did so much to popularise cocktails. During the golden age several classics were developed, including the Manhattan, the first named American cocktail to combine spirit and vermouth.

Vermouth, a fortified wine infused with herbs, spices, bark and seeds, had been used for centuries in Asia and Europe as a medicinal tincture. By the mid-eighteenth century, it was in demand as an aperitif in France, where a pale floral style was preferred, and Italy which favoured a red, sweeter version. Vermouth changed the flavour profile of mixed drinks and established a new category different to the snifters of yesteryear.

Cocktails were modern and they suited the progression of America from newly independent republic to burgeoning superpower where great cities were connected by railroads, and investors and industrialists conducted business and socialised in grand hotels, private clubs and restaurants.

WHO INVENTED
THE MARTINI?

Gin or vodka stirred with dry vermouth and ice, strained into a V-shaped stemmed glass and garnished with an olive or lemon twist. Clean, no-nonsense, elegant – that's a Martini. But who devised this iconic cocktail? No one knows because it appears to have evolved from a Manhattan (whiskey, sweet vermouth, bitters), which spawned the Martinez, described in a bar recipe book of 1884 as being like a Manhattan but with Old Tom gin or genever (both heavy and malty) instead of whiskey. Similar cocktails were referred to as Martena and Martine, but in 1887 the *Chicago Tribune* newspaper informed readers that, 'The Martini cocktail, made of vermouth, Booth's gin, and Angostura bitters is never so popular as at this season …' That version used sweet Italian vermouth, which is red and spicy, and Old Tom so it still resembled a Manhattan. By the time Frank Newman, bartender at the Paris Ritz, published a guidebook in 1904 the Dry Martini consisted of French (dry) vermouth, London dry gin, bitters and a lemon twist. When bitters left the recipe in the 1940s it was the cocktail we know today.

Creating cocktails was an art form, not casual drink wrangling, a profession that required training and knowledge. An edition of the weekly *Household Words* magazine in 1853 described barkeeps as accomplished artists, acrobats, magicians and conjurers as they threw glasses and tossed bottles. Those with the right skills, appearance and ability to mix a mean Martinez were in demand, and there were lucrative opportunities, especially for the bartenders who invented, claimed to have invented (hard to prove they did not) or were associated with specific cocktails.

To mix cocktails effectively, the appropriate toolkit is required. When the Boston shaker, consisting of two metal cups that fit neatly together, was introduced sometime before 1850, it added a note of theatre as the contents were vigorously shaken then strained into a glass. A shaker also altered the cocktail's mouthfeel and improved its flavour by intermingling the components, proving the mixologist's idiom, 'shake it to wake it'.

With the advent of steamships, nineteenth-century transatlantic crossings were quicker and easier than sail, and this encouraged travel between the USA and Europe and an exchange of ideas and social customs. Cocktails were *de rigueur* not only in America but across the pond in Britain, which had an active tippling culture, and they were established enough for Gin Twist (gin, hot water, lemon juice, sugar) to be mentioned by Sir Walter Scott in his 1823 novel *Saint Ronan's Well*. Medicinal potions had transformed into recreational beverages such as Pimm's No 1, a gin-based mixture with bitter herbs to aid digestion, and most famously Gin & Tonic, which was originally consumed by colonists and traders in tropical countries to prevent malaria. American author Mark Twain was convinced of the therapeutic benefits of one unnamed cocktail when he wrote to his wife from the UK and asked her to stock up with Scotch whisky, bitters, lemons and sugar on his return home. A doctor had prescribed that mixture as a digestif and instructed Twain to drink one before breakfast, dinner and bedtime. William Terrington's *Cooling Cups and Dainty Drinks*, published in 1869, was the original British

guidebook for libations. His gin cocktail, which could also be prepared with brandy, contained curaçao bitters, ginger syrup and ice, the tumbler rim moistened with lemon juice – a blend that would not be out of place on a modern menu.

The fact some mixologists are familiar to history, whereas those slinging beer and wine are not, suggests the creation of cocktails is exceptional. Jerry Thomas was a superstar and so were Harry Craddock and Harry MacElhone. The former Harry, a British-born US resident, tended bars at two of New York's luxury hotels, the Knickerbocker and Hoffman House, before fleeing Prohibition in 1926 and returning to his home country. Nicknamed 'the Dean of Cocktail Shakers', he was appointed as the Savoy Hotel's head barman and his *Savoy Cocktail Book* of 1930 (still in print) contains around 750 recipes from around the world, some of them his own formulation, so it acts as an archive of cocktails. Like Jerry Thomas, Craddock was adept at self-promotion, with tricks like announcing his return to work from holiday in a paid-for notice in London's *Times* newspaper.

Harry MacElhone, also British born, honed his craft at New York's Plaza Hotel, but earned renown at Ciro's Club in London and published in 1921 *Harry's ABC of Mixing Cocktails*. After he purchased a bar in Paris and renamed it Harry's New York Bar (still in business), Americans travelling in Europe or escaping Prohibition were unable to resist a visit to order one of his signature Sidecars.

Mixology as a noun has a modern feel, but it was already in use in 1898 when American Joseph L. Haywood published a cocktail book, *Mixology: The Art of Preparing all Kinds of Drinks*. The label 'mixologist' had been used with sarcasm decades earlier in New York's Knickerbocker magazine when a pretentious character in a short story styled the barman 'mixologist of tipulars'. Another description, possibly not sarcastic but grandiose, was in the *Montana Post* newspaper as 'mixologists of fluid excitements'. By the turn of the century 'mixologist' was a common description for the profession of cocktail making, and although H. L. Mencken, American essayist and cultural commentator, thought it pompous, he must surely have been grateful to

whoever rustled up the Martini he pronounced as 'the only American invention as perfect as the sonnet'.

Dale DeGroff, aka King Cocktail, legendary bartender, author and co-founder of the Museum of the American Cocktail, reclaimed the word 'mixologist' in the 1980s. He is acknowledged as the godfather of the modern cocktail renaissance for reviving late-nineteenth-century staples and reminding people about the flawlessness of a well-mixed Old Fashioned.

THE ICE MAN COMETH

Frederic Tudor is a footnote in history, but his nickname 'The Ice King' is apt recognition of his role in the progression of cocktails. Tudor was a Boston businessman who in 1806 had the idea of shipping blocks of ice from frozen Massachusetts lakes to warmer climes. Icehouses already existed in colonial America, mostly in regions with cold winters, where ice was used in food preservation and medicine. Frederic Tudor honed production techniques, built a distribution network, sold ice to India and the Caribbean, and became one of America's first millionaires. As prices decreased ice became commonplace in the USA and it was used to chill drinks, bringing refreshment and relief in scorching weather. There was no going back to tepid tipples, and when Jerry Thomas published *How to Mix Drinks, or The Bon Vivant's Companion* in 1862, the majority of recipes included ice.

THE GOLDEN AGE

AN AMERICAN ERA known as the Gilded Age between 1870 and the end of the century was a period of astonishing economic growth, particularly in northern and western states. This epoch partially coincided with the golden age of cocktails when smart hotels, private clubs and upmarket restaurants in major cities employed mixologists to create the liquid symbol of sophistication. Cocktails were so engrained in the affluent self-image of the USA that the American exhibition at the Paris World Fair 1867 featured a bar. Each day it sold Sherry Cobblers by the thousand (a long drink of sherry, citrus juice, sugar and crushed ice) to eager visitors. This launched a fascination with what the French termed *boissons américaines* and spurred the establishment of American Bars in European capitals, the first in London's Criterion restaurant.

Saloons in the USA were male spaces, and some states banned females from entering them. Women who did patronise bars were usually sex workers and judged by polite society as being morally deficient. As for cocktails,

they were the domain of men because spirits and bitters were deemed too manly and intense for the opposite sex, but were it not for women adopting them, they would not now have the status as a drink for all. *The New York Sun* newspaper reported on women in upmarket cafés ordering cocktails: '… and now they are coquetting with a subtle compound of gin and vermouth, which they call "the Martini".' That could refer to any modern city, but it was from an edition printed in 1887 and is significant because it suggests that sipping cocktails in public was already a fashionable activity for rebellious young urban females.

America was developing not just economically but societally too, and this was the era of the New Woman just two decades after the end of the Civil War, when campaigning in support of the abolition of slavery and, later, universal suffrage had given some women a public platform. In the largest cities a ponderous move towards equality had begun, with the relaxation of some social constraints, but it was a different story in small-town and rural America where life was more conservative, and people were expected to behave as conventions decreed. The beginning of protestant religious revivalism in the 1820s urged the faithful to become perfect humans, and churches championed an existing temperance movement that vilified the consumption of alcohol and promoted total abstinence. Due to the colonial history of rum, and settlers from Scotland and Ireland with their tradition of whisk(e)y, spirits were embedded in America's idea of itself. There were other reasons for their ubiquity: lack of easy access to beer as an alternative; the absence of breweries in rural areas; vast distances that made transportation of perishable beer impossible; and not least because high-strength liquor offered a significant bang for the buck. Drunkenness had been more acceptable in the eighteenth century, but in an industrialised nineteenth-century land that depended on a disciplined and productive workforce, it was not.

Even though most people were not excessive drinkers, alcoholism was a problem in some parts of society. It was not unknown for working-class men to spend their wage packets at the bar instead of on the family, leading to domestic violence and child poverty. The ensuing societal damage united

the Anti-Saloon League, Women's Christian Temperance Movement and Protestant churches, which together were an effective lobby in demonising drinking with slogans like: 'When the saloon goes, the devil will be ready to quit.' Over the decades, anti-alcohol zealots drew fervent political support for their crusade, and in 1919 they accomplished their goal when the National Prohibition Act was passed into law. Not only that but the US constitution was revised, with the Eighteenth Amendment stipulating:

> … the manufacture, sale, or transportation of intoxicating liquors within, the importation thereof into, or the exportation thereof from the United States and all territory

subject to the jurisdiction thereof for beverage purposes is hereby prohibited.

If only lawmakers had studied attempts by other countries to ban the booze, they would have realised it is impossible to stop an entire population from imbibing. As history proves, there is never a right time to restrict intoxicants, but in America the politicians had chosen an especially wrong time because this was post-First World War, and life was changing, especially for women. Many of the personnel, men *and* women, who returned from serving overseas had experienced new cultures and social freedoms, and after surviving the war to end all wars, supposedly fought for self-determination, their right to determine whether or not to have a snifter had been eliminated. Another significant post-war development was the Nineteenth Amendment to the constitution in 1920, which granted some women the right to vote. During America's short period fighting with the Allies, women had worked in many jobs temporarily vacated by men and they were increasingly emancipated. There was no going back.

With Prohibition, licensed premises ceased serving alcoholic drinks. In their place illicit speakeasies popped up, 32,000 in New York city alone, double the number of formerly legal venues. Some were cramped cellars, or backrooms, others more spacious and deluxe with bands, dancing and showgirls, and they turned into entertainment magnets. Three of them, the Cotton Club, El Morocco and the Stork Club, went on to be leading night spots. Speakeasies were clandestine and, with a whiff of danger, exciting. Many were integrated in a country where racial segregation was the law. This was the Jazz Age, with modern attitudes counter to the staid lifestyle promoted by evangelicals, especially those who espoused a ban on alcohol.

For independent women who were partial to a drink, Prohibition offered opportunities, not just for their social life, but with employment too. They were welcomed as paying customers, and to work as hostesses and bartenders. In some cases they owned the joint, running what were termed 'home speaks' serving homemade or smuggled hooch. As for bootlegging, the covert trade of distributing and selling spirits, more women than men were involved, leading to newspapers using the terms 'bootleggeress' or 'bootleggerette' to describe them, or the slang phrase 'snake charmer'. It was usually practised on a small scale in order to provide income for the women's families, but some, particularly the ones who had legal liquor businesses prior to Prohibition, amassed great wealth and earned nicknames like 'Moonshine Mary'.

Despite efforts by law enforcement to prevent the purchase of alcohol, anyone thirsty, particularly in a city, could easily find a snifter because in addition to hundreds of thousands of speakeasies across the land, drugstores, laundries, barbershops, tearooms and other places

surreptitiously sold it. Bootleg Scotch and Canadian whisky, smuggled into the country by rumrunners and usually distributed by organised crime, were available in some places, but more likely the accessible intoxicant was moonshine, or industrial spirit flavoured with juniper to resemble gin. Cocktails were a godsend because mixers masked the unpleasant flavours and burn of low-quality product. Speakeasies were at risk of being raided by federal agents, so the ideal cocktails were quick and simple to make – Bee's Knees with gin, lemon juice and honey, or Whiskey Rickey, a mix of bourbon, lime juice and soda water.

Prohibition had several unintended consequences, most notably an increase in criminality as bootlegging gangs fought for market share; and because hard liquor is concentrated alcohol and easier than wine and beer to transport and hide, consumption increased. Most spirits were quaffed at home, not in speakeasies, often after being prescribed by a friendly doctor who took advantage of the loophole that permitted certain distillers to sell whiskey for medicinal use.

Affluent Americans could escape on booze cruises in international waters, or to Cuba where white rum was queen, and mixologists in bars like the Hotel Sevilla were the kings shaking Mary Pickfords (white rum, pineapple juice, grenadine, Maraschino liqueur) or Daiquiris (white rum, lime juice, simple syrup). Alternatively, they travelled to Europe where some of America's top bartenders who had found sanctuary working in Paris and London were improving the cocktail menus of both cities.

Britain in the 1920s was party time for those with the inclination and wherewithal. The devil-may-care exuberance personified by the Charleston dance was a consequence of the misery and privations of the First World War followed by the global flu pandemic, together responsible for the death of millions of people. Married women over the age of 30 had been enfranchised in 1918 and a less restrictive era was dawning. This was reflected in flapper fashion, where young women abandoned corsets and wore

loose-fitting drop-waist dresses with raised hemlines, trousers, make-up, and shingled or cropped hair. Fun-loving bohemian aristocrats were known as the Bright Young Things and the popular media was obsessed with them. As with celebrities today, they warranted endless column inches and were trendsetters who influenced the public by what they wore, where they went and what they drank. And what did they drink? Cocktails of course! Gin & It at London's louche 43 Club, or a Hanky Panky at the Savoy.

Cocktail parties as pre-dinner rituals were the thing to do. Starting late afternoon for around ninety minutes, with drinks and light finger food, they were adopted wholeheartedly by the upper and aspiring classes of 1920s London. Alec Waugh, brother of English society novelist Evelyn, claimed to have conceived the format and maybe he was the person to introduce them in Britain, but in America, casual afternoon events in the home where men and women socialised with punch and wine cups were already the fashion. In 1917, wealthy St Louis socialite Clara Bell Walsh featured in newspapers when she hosted a party where her guests, women included, sipped stronger stuff. This was so newsworthy the *St. Paul Pioneer Press* described how the party was a draw for her fifty guests, and within weeks cocktail parties were a St Louis institution. *The Tacoma Times* stated: 'Positively the newest stunt in society is the giving of "cocktail parties" ... a Sunday matinee affair which originated here ... filling a long felt Sunday want in society circles ... Mrs. Walsh, because of her innovation has become more of a social celebrity in St. Louis than ever.'

In America the roaring-drunk twenties proved that the enforcement of Prohibition in such a vast country was unworkable, and it was repealed in 1933, appropriately by President Franklin D. Roosevelt, who liked to host a daily cocktail party and mix the Martinis himself. In his announcement he used the language of the organisations that had originally lobbied for Prohibition: 'I trust in the good sense of the American people that they will not bring upon themselves the curse of excessive use of intoxicating liquors, to the detriment of health, morals and social integrity.' What he failed to mention was that money, or lack of, was the motivation for the law change, because fourteen

years of absent tax receipts had drained the treasury and in the Great Depression the federal government could no longer afford to forego such easy income.

Merrymakers across the land flocked to 'Farewell to the Eighteenth Amendment' parties and raised a glass to liberty. A crowd of 10,000 in New York's Times Square roared at the illumination of an electric sign displaying the phrase, 'Prohibition is dead!' In photo after photo the revellers hold cocktails, and most of them are women. As

the *Chicago Tribune* reported, 'Women flock to bars as the new wet era opens. Many women are crowding up to be served, something considered not quite right in the days preceding Prohibition.'

An enduring legacy was the permanent change in habits, where women socialised in bars and moved into spaces previously limited to men. *American Vogue* magazine observed in the 1930s, 'After the War, but more particularly after Prohibition, girls and women began to drink. The lifting of a glass was, for a little while, one of the modern gestures.'

Prohibition made drinking fashionable, and the movies boosted that perception when Hollywood chose the cocktail as an emblem of glamour. Talking pictures had arrived.

COCKTAILS AND CULTURE

'AMMUNITION? HIGHBALLS and cocktails – the long and short of it.' That line was spoken by actor William Powell in *The Thin Man* (1934), the earliest Hollywood film where cocktails had a major role. Powell played Nick Charles, and he and his wife Nora (Myrna Loy) were the silver screen's most alluring couple. Wealthy, good-looking, with fabulous costumes, sparkling wit and comedy banter, they solved murder mysteries together. They also drank cocktails. A lot of cocktails.

Nora was a modern woman who enjoyed her drink, had fun with it, and matched her husband's intake. As a connoisseur, he instructed the barman in his mixing technique: 'The important thing is the rhythm. Always have rhythm in your shaking. Now a Manhattan you shake to foxtrot time, a Bronx to two-step time, but a Dry Martini you always shake to waltz time.' Filmgoers adored the glittering couple so much there were five sequels; the Nick & Nora Martini (a 3:1 ratio of gin to vermouth) was a hit, and home cocktail bars became the rage.

Hollywood conveyed the message that cocktails were stylish. They represented elegance and an enviable lifestyle and were associated with filmdom's biggest luminaries. In *Anna Christie*, silent movie icon Greta Garbo's first speaking role was hyped with the slogan 'Garbo Talks!' and her opening words were 'Gimme a whiskey, ginger ale on the side.' Claudette Colbert orders White Ladies in *It Happened One Night*; Ginger Rogers sips Bucks Fizz with Fred Astaire in *Top Hat*; Clark Gable and Constance Bennett spar over Martinis in *After Office Hours*; and in the 1937 film *Every Day's a Holiday*, Mae West drinks Bellinis, and a character utters the line, 'You should get out of those wet clothes and into a Dry Martini.'

Some of the most memorable scenes in classic films feature cocktails: Bette Davis as Margo Channing in *All About Eve* gulping down Gibsons and declaring, 'Fasten your seatbelts, it's going to be a bumpy night'; Marilyn Monroe's Sugar Kane in *Some Like It Hot* mixing Manhattans in a hot water bottle during a Prohibition-era train journey; and resistance fighter Victor Laszlo (Paul Henreid) ordering a Champagne cocktail at Rick's Café Américain in the film *Casablanca*.

As for cocktail parties, they were usually portrayed as the best time ever, as in *Auntie Mame* when the eponymous character serves her signature concoction 'Flaming Mame' and advises guests to 'Drink them up fast before the alcohol burns away'; the lavish gatherings thrown by ultra-rich bootlegger Jay Gatsby in *The Great Gatsby*, where the Gin Rickeys flow; and Holly Golightly's bash in *Breakfast at Tiffany's*, where dozens of strangers cram into her tiny apartment and swig so much liquor the local shop makes an emergency delivery, which she describes with relief as 'reinforcements'.

In some films, cocktails are symbols to represent foreplay, as they were for Humphrey Bogart and Lauren Bacall in most of their films (they were also romantically involved off-set); or rebellion, when in *Bonfire of the Vanities* someone banned from drinking because of ill-health orders Sidecars one after the other with fatal results; or foibles, as they are in *The Big Lebowski*, with The Dude, whose hobbies include drinking White Russians.

Hollywood's moving talking pictures established enduring archetypes. The wise-cracking dame on first-name terms with the barman, the brooding outlaw finding solace in a whiskey bottle, the debonair playboy wooing his romantic targets with French 75s. Movies were influential because they portrayed a way of life viewers aspired to, and it was no coincidence that in the 1930s cocktails were the up-to-the-minute social activity.

It was not only films where cocktails were emblematic. In novels they sometimes drove the plot, communicated personality traits, and even acted as 'how to make' manuals. This was particularly the case in Raymond Chandler's *The Long Goodbye*, where Philip Marlowe is introduced to the ideal Gimlet: 'half gin and half Rose's Lime Juice and nothing else'; and the Champagne cocktail recipe in *The Big Sleep*: 'The Champagne as cold as Valley Forge and about a third of a glass of brandy beneath it.'

Arguably the most enthusiastic description of a cocktail came from Charles Dickens, who himself was partial to punch and a Smoking Bishop (red wine, port, roasted citrus fruit, sugar and spices). During his inaugural American lecture tour in 1842, Dickens was introduced to unfamiliar potations, so when he described the enjoyment his hero had to one in *The Life and Adventures of Martin Chuzzlewit*, he was writing from experience:

Martin took the glass with an astonished look; applied his lips to the reed; and cast up his eyes once in ecstasy. He paused no more until the goblet was drained to the last drop. 'This wonderful invention, sir,' said Mark, tenderly patting the empty glass, 'is called a cobbler. Sherry cobbler when you name it long; cobbler, when you name it short.'

One cocktail more than any other – the Dry Martini – encourages rapture. The narrator in Ernest Hemingway's *A Farewell to Arms* eulogised, 'I had never tasted anything so cool and clean. They made me feel civilized'; essayist and wit Dorothy Parker famously wrote, 'I like to have a Martini, two at the very most. After three I'm under the table, after four I'm under my host'; and film director Alfred Hitchcock joked that his perfect Martini consisted of five parts gin and 'a short glance at a bottle of vermouth'. The most familiar fictitious Martini aficionado is, of course, James Bond. In the 1953 book *Casino Royale* he instructs the barman how to mix his version of a Martini, christened the Vesper after his *inamorata*, and it is served, on his orders, in a deep Champagne goblet, with three parts gin, one of vodka, vermouth, a thin slice of lemon peel, to be shaken not stirred. Bond was not the first to utter that phrase because Nick Charles in *The Thin Man* also said it, eschewing the stir in favour of a shake.

Martinis are undeniably stylish, urbane and anything but frivolous. Tipplers who preferred playfulness embraced the Tiki craze, which began in 1934 with the opening of Don the Beachcomber restaurant in Los Angeles, where the interior was a mishmash of bamboo partitions, barstools, fishing nets with glass weights draped on the walls, and palm tree fronds. Its extrovert owner, Ernest Gantt, a bootlegger during Prohibition, invented a new category of cocktails he titled Rhum Rhapsodies – more Caribbean than Polynesian – mixing rum, fresh juices and syrups, garnished with paper umbrellas and chunks of fruit, and presented in coconuts or hollowed pineapples. One of his creations, the Zombie, named according to legend because its super-strength turned people into the walking dead, contained three types of rum plus absinthe, grenadine, bitters and lime juice. Gantt kept his recipes a secret by giving them number references, and coding the ingredients to prevent plagiarism, but, despite that, Zombies were sold at New York's 1939 World Fair, where their invention was claimed by a bar owner called Monty Prosser.

Don the Beachcomber's escapism and fun was an idealised version of what Americans believed South Pacific culture to be, an antidote to the woes of the Great Depression. The format was a hit, especially with Hollywood celebrities, and spawned a copycat, Hinky Dinks, soon retitled Trader Vic's, in Oakland, California. Both Don the Beachcomber and Trader Vic's, owned by Victor Bergeron, were so successful that sites opened in other American cities, and the latter internationally following a deal with Hilton hotels.

Perhaps the best-known Tiki cocktail is the Mai Tai, consisting of dark rum, orange curaçao, lime juice and

The Vermouth from which the "Martini Cocktail" derives its name.

simple syrup, but who conceived it? Gantt and Bergeron both asserted it was them, with Bergeron becoming especially indignant if anyone doubted his ownership, describing how a Tahiti-resident friend took a sip of his new mixture and commented, '*Mai Tai-Roa Aé*', which roughly translates as 'out of this world'. Historians believe it was more likely to have been Gantt who, over his career, devised many cocktails, including Three Dots and a Dash – Morse code for the letter 'V' – which celebrated Allied victory in the Second World War.

Tiki culture had a significant boost with San Francisco's Golden Gate International Exposition 1939, which included the 'Pageant of the Pacific' celebrating Polynesia. Military personnel returning after the war from serving in the South Pacific brought home souvenirs and stories of their experiences overseas, and by the 1950s, tiki influences were in architecture, interior design, home décor and clothing. The US economy was thriving, and life was good for millions of Americans. Tiki culture was joyful, innocent, and represented an easy-going existence with a soundtrack of ukulele music. Hawaii, which in 1959 became the USA's fiftieth state, was a leading holiday destination, and the flocks of tourists could sip Blue Hawaii cocktails – white rum, vodka, blue curaçao, pineapple juice, served long and garnished with a paper umbrella and pineapple wedge – on beautiful sunny beaches. America's Tiki craze ended with war in Vietnam, although advocates of kitsch keep it alive to this day, and it returned as a retro lifestyle with the Rockabilly revival in the late 70s.

Cocktails were uncool with the youthful followers of the 1960s counter-culture movement, when recreational drugs were the chosen method for a buzz. Mixed drinks were passé because that's what the parents drank with their friends, and they were associated with strait-laced businessmen meeting clients for the euphemistic three-Martini lunch. But when in 1988 the film *Cocktail* was released, highlighting the entertaining techniques of flair bartending,

IT IS MY PLEASURE TO OFFER YOU THESE DRINKS. SOME I HAVE GATHERED AT THEIR ORIGIN AND OTHERS ARE MY OWN CONCOCTIONS.

RUM KEG
(for four persons) 5.25
A delightful barrel full of Rums, Liqueurs and fresh fruit juices

KAVA BOWL (for four persons) . 5.25
Light and aromatic rums, fruit juices, Grenadine and Liqueurs, served in a communal bowl with 20-inch straws

SCORPION (for four persons) . 5.25
A festive concoction of Rums, Fruit Juices and Brandy, with a whisper of Almond, bedecked with Gardenias and served with long straws

**TRADER VIC'S
RUM CUP** (for two) 3.75
A frosty froth of fine Rums, Orange, Lemon and Lime with Liqueurs, served in a Scorpion Bowl

TIKI BOWL 2.50
A delightful punch served in earthen bowl supported by three Tikis—replicas of authentic Tahitian gods

TRADER VIC'S DAIQUIRI . . 1.75
A frosted version

SIBONEY 1.25
A great Caribbean cocktail named after the original Siboney Indians

SIEGERT'S BOUQUET . . . 1.25
Siegert's Rum of Trinidad and a blending of liqueurs with Lemon make this a tart yet sweet cocktail

TRADER VIC'S COCKTAIL . . 1.25
A simple rum cocktail

BACARDI 1.25
Bacardi at its best . . . with Lime and Grenadine

BARBADOS COCKTAIL . . . 1.25
A Daiquiri made with fine Barbados Rum

GIMLET . . 1.25
Dry Gin and Roses Lime Juice . . . a Monk Antrim Special

HONOLULU 1.75
The Drink of the Islands . . . a smooth concoction of Rum and Pineapple with a lemon accent

JAMAICA FLOAT 1.25
For devotees of fine Jamaica Rum

KONA GOLD 1.25
A frosty presentation of fine Jamaica Rum

LA FLORIDA 1.35
A subtly flavored light Rum Cocktail from La Florida Bar in Havana

a generation who had no memory of such libations were intrigued, and the resurgence began. The lounge- and swing-music rebirth of the 1990s celebrated a 'cool' version of American life, and this was reflected by the movie *Swingers*, with a plotline about the social lives of struggling actors in Los Angeles. Scenes were filmed in an extant old-school bar, the Dresden Room, and the marketing poster featured a photo of the star holding a Martini headlined with the slogan 'Cocktails first ... questions later.'

Popular culture has always influenced attitudes, behaviour and motivations. Early Hollywood glamorised cocktails, and television continued the trendsetting role. *Mad Men* was an ultra-stylish period drama ostensibly about New York City's advertising industry from the 1960s to 1970s, but as the executives were rarely seen without a glass in their hands, it was really about cocktails. Whiskey Sours, Gimlets, Gibsons, Manhattans and Martinis all feature prominently, but none more so than the Old Fashioneds regularly sipped in moody bars by charismatic main character Don Draper. Another seminal TV series, *Sex and the City*, is inextricably linked with a specific cocktail: the Cosmopolitan. The show, revolutionary at the time, tells the stories of four single career women in 1990s New York, traversing the city on their terms, in and out of fashionable venues with the freedom to do what they wanted and when. They liked a nip, and the Cosmo, as it was labelled, appeared frequently, symbolising their

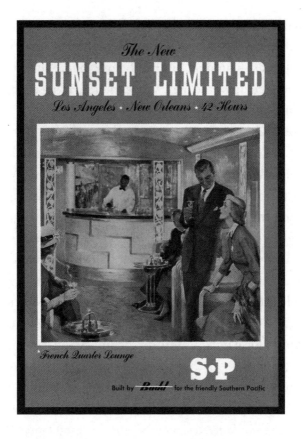

The New
SUNSET LIMITED
Los Angeles · New Orleans · 42 Hours

French Quarter Lounge

S·P

Built by *Budd* for the friendly Southern Pacific

independence, tight friendship and good taste. It was
the zeitgeist cocktail of the 90s, a tangy fusion of vodka,
Cointreau, fresh lime and cranberry juice, devised in 1988
by Toby Cecchini, bartender of the hip Odeon restaurant
in downtown Manhattan's Tribeca district. The instantly
recognisable pink triangle in the V-shaped Martini glass
was the crucial element because people wanted to be seen

with it. *Sex and the City* introduced the Cosmopolitan to an international audience and it was like a gateway drug where people start with one thing and move on to more potent highs, but in this case they were exploring other speciality cocktails and heralding an age of rediscovery.

Social media did not exist in the 1990s but if it had, *SATC*'s Carrie would likely have used it to chronicle her life, including photographing what she was drinking. Visual appeal is what makes cocktails such stars on Instagram and photo-led websites, causing viewers to yearn for the experience hinted at in the picture and drink them in real life. The worldwide web begat worldwide demand and now almost every global city has fabulous bars where mixologists not only create the classics but devise their own signature cocktails, sometimes foraging for ingredients or mixing in local botanicals to give their handiwork a unique selling point.

The glamour of cocktails is a major reason for their enduring appeal. Of all intoxicating beverages they lend themselves to fantasies, whether that is being James Bond nonchalantly ordering a Vodka Martini, or the captivating fifties screen goddess Ava Gardner sipping a Daiquiri. But more than anything, they make us feel good, and right from the beginning of humans' love affair with alcohol, that has been the real motivator.

THE COCKTAIL MENU

THIS IS A recipe collection of some of the best-loved classic cocktails, one from each of the world's major spirits, with details of their origins.

Whether a cocktail is shaken or stirred during preparation depends on its components. Blends of liquor alone are better stirred; those with cream, syrup, fruit juice, and anything with a thicker texture need a vigorous shake to ensure they are fully mixed.

Some of these recipes include liquid sugar, known in mixology as simple syrup. To make it, gently heat 100 grams of sugar in a saucepan with 50 ml water, stir and bring to the boil until the sugar has dissolved, then leave to cool before using it.

ABSINTHE

Death in the Afternoon

This aniseed-flavoured Champagne cocktail was devised by author Ernest Hemingway after his novel of the same name, published in 1932. Hemingway's instructions were: 'Pour one jigger absinthe into a Champagne glass. Add iced Champagne until it attains the proper opalescent milkiness. Drink three to five of these slowly.'

Opalescence, dubbed the 'louche' effect, is caused by the emulsification that happens when watery liquids are added to absinthe.

Ingredients
30 ml absinthe
5 ml simple syrup (see page 79)
125 ml Champagne or other sparkling wine
Twist of lemon

Method
Pour the absinthe and simple syrup into a chilled glass and stir. Top up with the sparkling wine. For the lemon garnish, wash the fruit to remove wax or pesticides from the skin. Use a vegetable peeler to cut a long piece of zest without the pith. Twist to a curl by hand and float on top of the cocktail.

Glassware
Flute

BRANDY

Sidecar

An orange-flavoured cocktail, possibly named after a motorcycle sidecar. It appeared in print in 1922 and was credited as the invention of Pat McGarry, bartender at London's Buck's Club, and then popularised at Harry's New York Bar in Paris.

Ingredients
50 ml Cognac
25 ml triple sec
25 ml freshly squeezed lemon juice
Twist of lemon or orange

Method
Fill a cocktail shaker with ice cubes. Pour in the liquids and shake, then strain into a chilled glass. Float the twist on top of the cocktail, to garnish.

Glassware
Coupe

GIN

French 75

This was initially called the *Soixante Quinze* for the French 75-millimetre field gun so effective during the First World War. It evolved from an earlier cocktail that might also have contained apple brandy.

Ingredients

2 teaspoons simple syrup (see page 79)
25 ml London dry gin
15 ml freshly squeezed lemon juice
Champagne or sparkling wine, to taste
Twist of lemon

Method

Pour the simple syrup over ice in a cocktail shaker, followed by the gin and lemon juice. Shake vigorously, then strain into a flute, top up with Champagne and gently stir. Garnish with the twist of lemon.

Glassware

Flute

RUM

Daiquiri

Daiquiri, after a Cuban mining town, is a cocktail from the late-nineteenth century. The classic version is made of white rum, lime juice and syrup. A frozen version also contains fruit purée and crushed ice and resembles a slushy.

Ingredients

50 ml white rum
25 ml freshly squeezed lime juice
10 ml simple syrup (see page 79)
Wheel of lime

Method

Combine the liquid ingredients with ice in a cocktail shaker and shake vigorously. Strain into a chilled glass and garnish with a wheel of lime hooked on the rim.

Glassware

Martini

RON

DAIQUIRI

COCTELERA

COCKTAIL | BOOK

MARCA REGISTRADA

COMPAÑIA

RON DAIQUIRI S.A.

HABANA —— CUBA

TEQUILA

Margarita

Like many cocktails, this Mexican classic has several origin stories. Most plausible is that it was a version of a Daisy (*margarita* is Spanish for 'daisy'), where any spirit is combined with citrus juice and grenadine and served over shaved ice. In 1948 it became Mexico's official drink. A salted rim is a personal choice and only necessary if the tequila is rough stuff, because salt diminishes harshness.

Ingredients

35 ml tequila
15 ml triple sec
20 ml freshly squeezed lime juice
10 ml simple syrup (see page 79)
Wedge(s) of lime
Salt (optional)

Method

Place the liquid ingredients into a cocktail shaker with ice, shake, then strain into a glass. To salt the glass, rub a slice of lime around the rim, then roll the rim at an angle over a saucer of table salt – the angle helps prevent the salt from sticking to the inside of the glass. Garnish with a lime wedge.

Glassware

Coupe

VODKA

Black Russian

A vodka cocktail attributed to Gustave Tops, bartender at Brussels' Hotel Metropole, who initially prepared it in 1949 for Perle Mesta, the American ambassador to Luxembourg.

Ingredients
50 ml vodka
25 ml coffee liqueur
2 maraschino cherries

Method
Pour the vodka and coffee liqueur into a tumbler filled with ice and stir. Garnish with a couple of maraschino cherries on a cocktail stick dipped in the drink.

Glassware
Tumbler

WHISKEY

MANHATTAN

Named after the New York City island, this dates from at least 1882 but where it was created is unknown. Both the Manhattan Club and Hoffman House hotel claimed it as their own.

INGREDIENTS
75 ml rye whiskey
25 ml sweet vermouth
A dash of bitters
3 maraschino cherries

METHOD
Combine the liquids in a cocktail shaker or mixing glass with ice cubes and stir. Strain into a glass and garnish with the cherries on a cocktail stick balanced across the rim.

GLASSWARE
Coupe

THE GARNISH GAME

No cocktail is complete without a garnish. They are the finishing touch. They do not just add visual appeal with flair, drama and a decorative element but, if edible, infuse the drink with extra flavour or aroma. The most widespread garnishes are:

CITRUS WEDGE, WHEEL, TWIST: used in numerous cocktails including the Negroni. Citrus adds acidity, liveliness and essential oils. For added zest, rub the peel around the rim of the glass.

CHERRIES: add a hint of sweetness, especially to bitter cocktails, but also enhance fruity cocktails like Piña Colada.

OLIVES: impart saltiness and savoury notes to earthy cocktails. They give a hint of colour to the pure, clean visual aesthetic of a Martini.

VEGETABLES: an onion in a Gibson adds a savoury element, and a celery stick in a Bloody Mary lightens the sticky nature of tomato juice with its astringency.

HERBS: add flavour, aromatics, texture and crisp freshness. They need to be hand-smacked to liberate essential oils. Think mint leaves in a Mai Tai.

SALT: enhances fruit flavours in a drink such as the Paloma.

SPICES: complement the flavours of the cocktail, as cinnamon does when grated over the surface of a Brandy Alexander.

SUGAR: the rim of the glass is dipped in sugar crystals. For a tangy cocktail like the Lemon Drop the sweetness is a contrast.

And what of inedible garnishes? Plastic swizzle sticks, paper umbrellas and colourful straws date from the 1930s with the US craze for Polynesian-themed Tiki bars and cocktails.

GLOSSARY OF TERMS

ABV Alcohol by volume, a standard measurement of pure ethanol alcohol in 100 ml of liquid expressed as a percentage.

Apéritif/Aperitivo French and Italian (used in English) for an alcoholic drink taken before a meal to stimulate the appetite.

Base Spirit The alcoholic foundation of a cocktail. For example, gin in a Bramble.

Bitters High-alcohol concentrate infused with herbs, spices and other botanicals. Added to cocktails to enhance flavour or for balance.

Cordial Non-alcoholic flavoured syrup.

Digestif/Digestivo French and Italian (used in English) for an alcoholic drink consumed after a meal to aid digestion.

Dry Absence of sweetness.

Infusion When botanicals are infused for weeks in a spirit, their flavour intensifies. Some flavoured vodkas are infusions.

Jigger Bar tool used to measure the volume of liquids. Often shaped like an hourglass or an eggcup.

Liqueur Neutral distillate infused with botanicals and then sweetened. The name liqueur derives from the Latin *liquifacere*, which means to liquefy or dissolve. Liqueurs include Cointreau and Chartreuse.

Long Drink Usually a spirit and mixer with ice and garnish in a tall glass.

Maceration The process of soaking botanicals in liquid for a period to extract flavour.

Mixer A non-alcoholic liquid used to lengthen a drink; for instance fruit juice and tonic water.

Mocktail A non-alcoholic cocktail.

Muddle The action of crushing solid ingredients to release flavour and essential oils, the way mint leaves are for a Mojito.

Neat A measure of spirit served straight from the bottle without a mixer or ice.

On the Rocks A measure of spirit or a cocktail over ice.

Proof A measure of the amount of alcohol. Proof is double the percentage of alcohol by volume, so 40 per cent ABV is 80 per cent proof.

Served Long Over ice in a tall glass with more volume of mixer than spirit.

Shaken A cocktail with liquids of different viscosities, such as liquor and cream, or liquor and fruit juice, needs shaking in a cocktail shaker to fuse the ingredients together.

Shaker A metal, glass or plastic vessel for shaking cocktail ingredients.

Soda Water Artificially carbonated water, used as a mixer in some cocktails.

Stirred Blends of different alcohols that contain no juice, syrup or cream are stirred to mix them rather than shaken.

Straight Up A drink stirred with ice in a mixing vessel and strained into a glass.

Swizzle Stick A plastic or metal bar tool with several fingers at the end of the shaft, used for stirring. Swizzle sticks were initially twigs from a native Caribbean tree used to stir the Swizzle beverage (a rum cocktail made with citrus, pineapple juice and bitters over crushed ice).

Tonic Water Artificially carbonated water infused with botanicals and used as a mixer.

Twist A piece of citrus peel (without the pith) floated on the surface of a cocktail as a garnish.

Virgin A non-alcoholic version of a cocktail.

Wheel A narrow disc of citrus fruit used as a garnish.

Zest The oily aromatic peel of citrus fruit added to cocktails for extra oomph.

COCKTAIL FORMATS

SOME COCKTAILS are templates that are modified by the choice of liquor.

COBBLER Fortified wine, or a base spirit, sweetened with simple syrup, in a long glass with crushed ice and garnished with a slice of orange or other fruit. Sherry Cobbler in one iteration.

COLLINS A sour cocktail with a base spirit, fresh lemon juice, simple syrup and soda water, served long over ice. Tom Collins with Old Tom gin is the most familiar.

FIZZ Sweet-sour cocktail from a base spirit, fresh citrus juice, simple syrup, and topped with soda water. Mojito is part of this family.

FLIP Contains fortified wine or a base spirit, plus sugar, and a whole egg. Brandy Flip is a popular choice.

Highball A spirit over ice with a carbonated mixer in a tall glass of the same name. The ubiquitous Gin & Tonic is a highball.

Rickey Any preferred spirit, fresh lime juice and soda water. Gin Rickey is well known.

Sling Served in a tall glass with any choice of spirit, fresh lemon juice, simple syrup, and sometimes carbonated water. For example, a Cape Cod.

Smash Consists of a spirit, simple syrup, fresh fruit, herbs and crushed ice. Rum Smash, for example.

Sour A sour contains spirit, lemon or lime juice and simple syrup; for instance a Whiskey Sour.

COCKTAIL PLACE NAMES

On the world map of named drinks, New York is the epicentre, with cocktails titled after four of its five boroughs. Most familiar is the Manhattan, made of rye whiskey, sweet vermouth and bitters. In addition there are:

☞ Bronx: gin, sweet vermouth, dry vermouth, orange juice

☞ Brooklyn: whiskey, dry vermouth, maraschino liqueur, bitters

☞ Queens: gin, sweet vermouth, dry vermouth, pineapple juice

So far, Staten Island has no cocktail, but there is Long Island Iced Tea, which contains no tea and is a melange of tequila, vodka, rum, triple sec, gin, simple syrup and cola. Other American city cocktails include:

☞ Chicago Fizz: white rum, tawny port, lemon juice, simple syrup, egg white

☞ Miami Beach: gin, pineapple juice, simple syrup

☞ San Francisco: vodka, triple sec, banana liqueur, grenadine, orange juice, pineapple juice

☞ Boston Tea Party: tequila, vodka, whiskey, rum, gin, dry vermouth, triple sec, orange juice, lime juice, simple syrup, cola (no tea!)

And while New Orleans, with its reputation for revelry, has no eponymous cocktail, it is dubbed 'the cradle of civilized drinking' from where several notable libations hail. Here is a selection:

☞ Sazerac (the official cocktail of Louisiana): absinthe, rye whiskey, Cognac, simple syrup, bitters

☞ Brandy Crusta: Cognac, orange curaçao, maraschino liqueur, lemon juice, simple syrup, bitters

☞ Hurricane: light rum, dark rum, passion fruit juice, orange juice, lime juice, simple syrup, grenadine

☞ Ramos Gin Fizz: gin, whipped cream, egg white, lemon juice, lime juice, orange flower water, soda water

☞ Vieux Carré: rye whiskey, Cognac, sweet vermouth, Bénédictine, bitters

☞ Café Brûlot Diabolique: a flaming concoction of Cognac, coffee and spices

☞ À La Louisiane: rye whiskey, Cognac,
   sweet vermouth, Bénédictine, bitters

And world cities too are celebrated in the cocktail
hall of fame with:

☞ The Parisian: gin, dry vermouth, crème
   de cassis
☞ Moscow Mule: vodka, lime juice, simple
   syrup, ginger beer
☞ London Fog: London dry gin, absinthe,
   simple syrup
☞ Singapore Sling: gin, cherry brandy,
   lemon juice, soda water

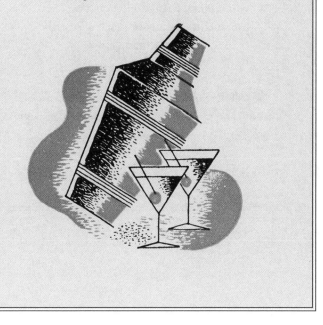

Finally, if anywhere deserves a celebratory cocktail, Brighton on England's south coast does. Brighton is an open-minded party town, always up for fun, and now it has its own cocktail, which I developed for this book. Mint is included for its enlivening ability and to settle the stomach after gorging on fish and chips!

THE CHEEKY

INGREDIENTS
50 ml Brighton Gin (Seaside Strength)
10 ml crème de menthe
100 ml cold peppermint tea
1 teaspoon seawater or pinch of sea salt
Mint, to garnish

METHOD
Stir all the liquids with a stick of seaside rock (candy) and serve over ice in a Highball glass with a sprig of mint.

FURTHER READING

Cheryl Charming, *The Cocktail Companion* (Mango
    Publishing, 2018)
Harry Craddock, *The Savoy Cocktail Book* (Girard &
    Stewart, 2015)
Patrick E. McGovern, *Uncorking the Past* (University of
    California Press, 2009)
Jane Peyton, *The Philosophy of Gin* (British Library, 2020)
Mark Ridgwell, *Spirits Distilled* (Infinite Ideas, 2016)

LIST OF ILLUSTRATIONS

All images from the collections of the British Library unless otherwise stated.

Also available in this series

THE PHILOSOPHY OF
WHISKY
BILLY ABBOTT

THE PHILOSOPHY OF
CURRY
SEJAL SUKHADWALA
BRITISH LIBRARY

THE PHILOSOPHY OF
WINE
RUTH BALL

THE PHILOSOPHY OF
TEA
TONY GEBELY

THE PHILOSOPHY OF
GIN
JANE PEYTON

THE PHILOSOPHY OF
CHEESE
PATRICK McGUIGAN

THE PHILOSOPHY OF
BEER
JANE PEYTON

THE PHILOSOPHY OF
TATTOOS
JOHN MILLER

THE PHILOSOPHY OF
COFFEE
BRIAN WILLIAMS
BRITISH LIBRARY